Kotlin Development for Android (Create Your Own App)

by Michael J. Fordham

2017

Table of Contents

Chapter 6 – Extras

- Designing for different screen orientations

- Using your own app icon

Chapter 7 – Conclusion

- Overview of skills learnt

- Source code download

Chapter 1 - Intro to Kotlin

Kotlin is an exciting new programming language (1.0 release in February 2016)[1], which - at Google's 2017 I/O event for developers - was given the green light to become a first-class programming language for the Android platform, joining Java and C++.

What has people intrigued with the Kotlin language is that it is 100% interoperable with Java, and can run on the Java Virtual Machine (JVM), meaning any platform that can run Java should theoretically run Kotlin too. This special relationship with Java is also a major bonus for programmers who already know how to code in Java, as the languages aren't too dissimilar, with Kotlin actually being easier to learn and requiring around 40% less lines of code to do the same things as Java code would, according to JetBrains[1], the developers of the language.

For example, below is an example of how you could write a "hello world" program in Java, and then in Kotlin:

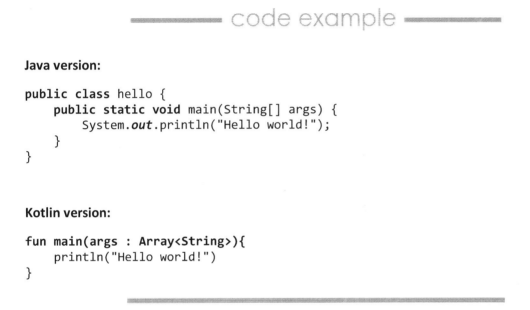

Java version:

```java
public class hello {
    public static void main(String[] args) {
        System.out.println("Hello world!");
    }
}
```

Kotlin version:

```kotlin
fun main(args : Array<String>){
    println("Hello world!")
}
```

As you can see, the same program requires 2 less lines of code in the Kotlin variant, and does not require you to make it in a class, being as you don't need to necessarily. You can also see that some steps have been shortened, like writing to the console no longer requires *System.out.println* and then a semicolon at the end of the line from Java, as you can now do this with a more straightforward *println* in Kotlin.

Another thing to note when developing with Kotlin is that you can have inferred data types with variables, meaning the compiler decides what the data type the variable should be when the program compiles, based on the data assigned to the variable. So, for example, in Java we could define variables with their data type, followed by their name, and you could either assign them a value or leave them null. This would then be followed by a semicolon to end the line of code. In Kotlin, we simply state that we are creating a variable, and then the name of the variable, followed by a value or the data type and question mark if we are leaving it null. Examples of this can be seen below.

———————— code example ————————

Java version:

```
int number = 0;
```

Kotlin version:

```
var number = 0
var nullNumber: Int?
```

Variables can be either mutable or immutable in Kotlin, meaning in layman's terms whether or not their value can be changed after they have been assigned a value. If you wish to make a mutable (i.e. changeable) variable, you use the *var* keyword, and if you wish to make an immutable (i.e. non-changeable) variable, you use the *val* keyword.

That's enough for the explanation of why Kotlin is going to be a great language for you to get your teeth into now though, as we can move on to downloading and setting up *Android Studio*, so you can start building your app!

Chapter 2 – Android Studio 3.0 Set-Up

To develop an Android app, you will need an IDE which supports Android development. There are a few that do, including Android Studio and IntelliJ IDEA. For the duration of this book, we will be using Android Studio 3.0. This is the first version of Android Studio to support Kotlin straight out the box. So, to download this the latest version of Android Studio, go here: http://bit.ly/2AokPjC

Once you have downloaded Android Studio, you can run through the installation process to quickly set up the IDE. Follow the on-screen tips to help you get this done properly.

Before you begin creating apps, you may need to install a Java Development Kit (JDK) on your computer. You can get that here: http://bit.ly/2tVUAxa

You may also need to download an SDK (Software Development Kit) for an Android device if you wish to use an emulator to test the app on. SDKs can be downloaded from within Android Studio, using the download button in the top right of the screen with the Android head in front of it. You can also use your own Android device to test apps. On my end, I will be using a *OnePlus 3*, however you can use pretty much any device you like, so long as it runs Android. To do this however, you will need to follow these steps:

1. Go to Settings and then *About Phone* or *About Tablet* on your device (if you have Android 4.2 or higher)
2. Tap on the *Build Number* seven times, this activates *Developer Options* on your device
3. Go back to the Settings screen and scroll down, you will now see *Developer Options*

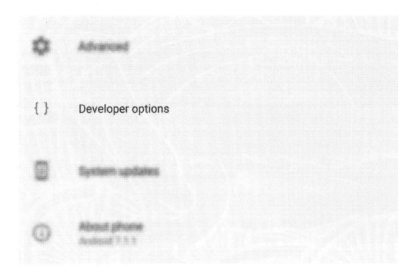

4. Inside this, scroll down to *USB debugging* and turn it on, you will see a confirmation message, tap OK.
5. Note: you may also be required to turn on *'Unknown sources'* under *Security* in order for your app to be installed on your device.

Now your device is ready to be used to test your apps on. To do this, you will need to plug your phone/tablet into your PC with a USB cable.

If you are missing any components, Android Studio will alert you to this and then give you the option to download the solutions and install them itself, without you having to do much more than wait while it executes its tasks.

Now we have the latest version of Android Studio set up, we can begin creating our first app in the next chapter.

Chapter 3 – Hello World! (Your First App)

A typical ritual when creating your first program or app in any language or platform, is to create one which simply prints out the words "hello world!" to the console. In Chapter 1, you saw how we can write a really simple *hello world* program in Java and Kotlin. Now however, we are going to do it in app-form.

Our first step, is creating a new project in Android Studio, so what you need to do is click *File, New, New Project*, and under the application name, we'll name it something like *'KotlinHelloWorld'*. You will notice on this screen, there is a checkbox for 'include Kotlin support', we want to tick that and press 'Next'.

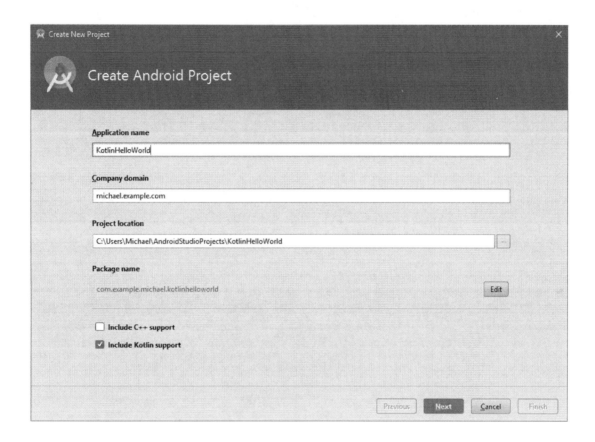

Now, we'll select the target Android devices we are going to be developing for. For now, we can leave 'Phone and Tablet' ticked, and you can choose the target API (Application Programming Interface). For the duration of this book, we'll be using *'API 16: Android 4.1 (Jelly Bean)'*. Click Next.

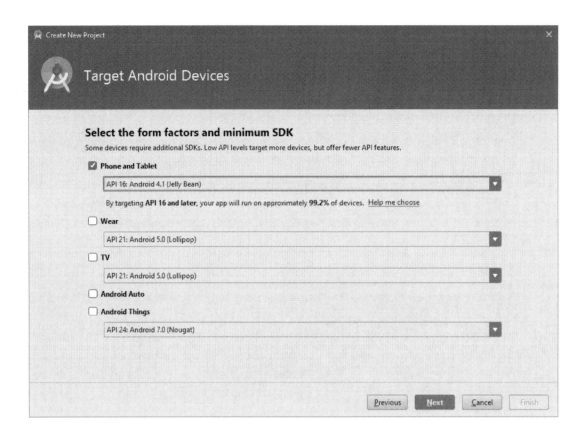

Now, we have to select the activity for the application. A typical application is made up of many activities, and we'll cover how you can add more than one activity to your app later on, but for now just select the 'Empty Activity' and click Next.

Finally, we have to select what to name the activity. For now, we can leave it as the '*MainActivity*', and have 'Generate Layout File', along with 'Backwards Compatibility' checked. Click Finish.

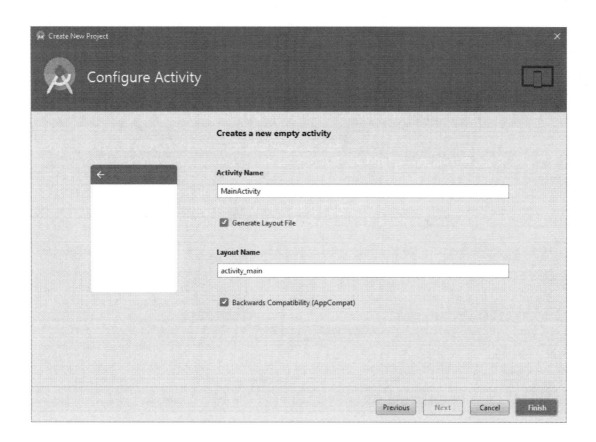

After the project has finished creating itself, you will be presented with a blank grey screen. You will want to open the project view, which you can do by clicking the '*1: Project*' button on the left sidebar of the screen.

Now, the sidebar on the left will likely show you some files and the main activity code screen should be shown too, however, we want to view the actual project folder on the left, so click the drop-down list as shown and select '*Project*'.

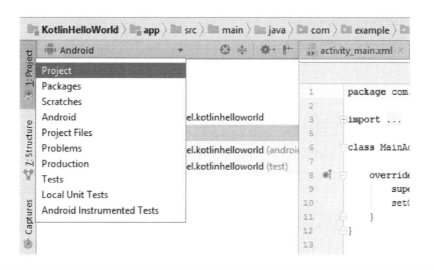

Once this view has been opened, we can select *KotlinHelloWorld, app, src, main,* and *java* to open the main activity or *res, layout* to open the design view of the main activity.

Once you are on the XML design view you will be presented with a screen like this:

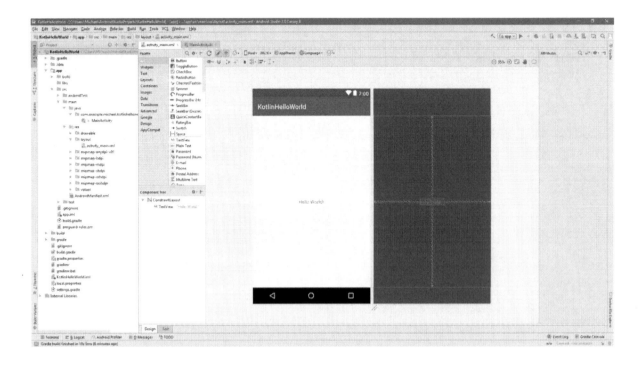

You can toggle between the XML code of the design and the actual design view of the app in the bottom menu.

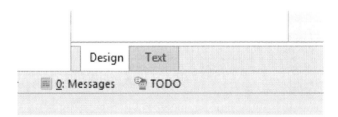

For now though, we will only deal with the design view. On your screen you may see 'Hello world!' already written. This is not the app we are building (sorry to disappoint, I know it could be the next big thing in the *Play Store*), so we are going to select that component and press delete (on your keyboard).

From here, we are going to drag a '*Button*' onto the screen of the device. In the '*Palette*' menu to the left of the design, we can see we have a number of components we can use in our app. Click the button option and drag it onto the screen.

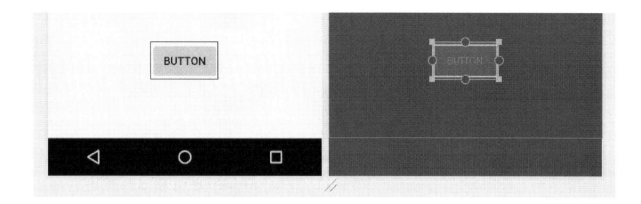

Now, on the right panel on-screen, '*Attributes*', we can see the properties of the component we have selected. With the button selected, we should name it something sensible and meaningful, like *btnSayHello*.

Note: When declaring names for components, variables and methods, 'camel case' notation is used, so instead of having a name like 'Btnsayhello' we have 'btnSayHello'. This makes our code easier to read. In addition, *classes* are supposed to have an upper-case first letter, so this notation helps us define what is a *class* and what is a *variable*, *component* or *method*.

So, in the ID box, type in '*btnSayHello*', then hit enter on your keyboard. You can also change the text of the button, so instead of saying 'Button', let's have it read 'Say Hello'. You can do this by editing the '*text*' attribute property in the same menu you edited the ID.

If you have completed the steps above you should now be left with a button which looks like this:

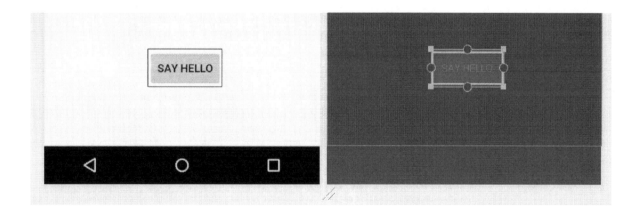

Now we can add another component to the screen, a *TextView*. This will allow us to show text on the app and also do stuff to the text when we click the button. So, now you will have to click and drag a 'TextView' to the app's screen.

Now that we have the TextView on screen, we can edit its attributes just like we could with the button on the right side of the screen. For this, we could name it '*lblText*' (lbl standing for label), and change the text of it to 'This is a test'.

You should have something on screen which looks like this:

Now, to make sure the components we have put on screen stay in place, we will need to start adding some *constraints* to the layout of the app. With the *button*, we can click and drag the circles on both sides of it when it is selected to either side of the screen, and this will hold it in place centrally.

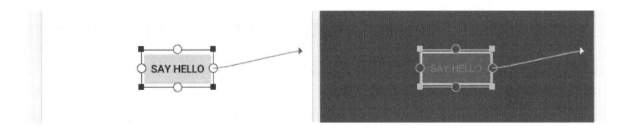

Once you have done this on both sides, you should end up with the *button* on screen looking like this:

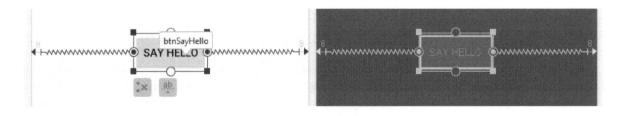

That jagged line indicates a connection to both sides of the screen, and as the connection is equal either side, the button should be centralised (this will differ on different devices occasionally as Android Studio likes to play with you mentally, so you may have to do some fiddling with it). Next, we will make a constraint with the bottom edge of the screen, by clicking and dragging the bottom circle of the button to the lower edge of the screen, like so:

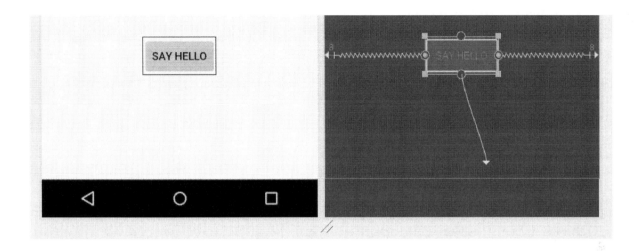

You will notice the button jumps to the bottom when you make the constraint, but you can edit how high it is with the attributes menu on the right, like so:

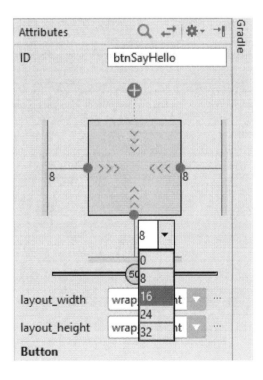

You can type in any value you like, or select the options from the drop-down list. We will be selecting '16' for now.

Now, we want to repeat the steps we performed for centralising the button, for the *TextView*, by dragging the circles on either side to the edges of the screen. Then, we will drag the bottom circle of the TextView to the top circle of the button, to create a constraint relationship between them. You should end up with something like this:

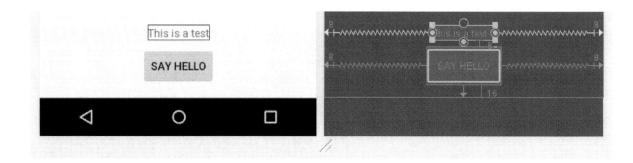

Of course, we don't want the components to be that close, so we can either edit the bottom margin of the TextView component in the attributes menu like we did with the button, or we can simply drag the TextView component up the screen away from the button. You should now have something like this:

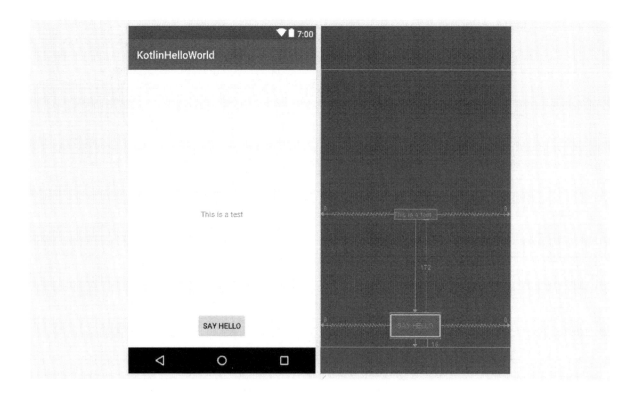

Now, we can start getting down to the actual programming aspect of this application, and help you code your first Android app.

Now, to start programming your app in Kotlin, you'll want to go back to the *MainActivity.kt* file which should be open in the tab bar at the top of your screen. You will see some code has already been generated. You will also notice the *onCreate* method. Code inside this method is run as soon as the app is started up.

What we're going to do is add a function to this code so that we can click the button we have placed on screen and then display different text on our TextView element.

Firstly however, we are going to bring a Kotlin library named *Anko* into our project, which will make interacting with our elements much easier. We are going to copy the line of code:

```
compile "org.jetbrains.anko:anko-commons:$anko_version"
```

We will then replace $anko_version with the build number that *Anko* is currently on. At the time of writing this book, *Anko* was on 0.10.1 (you can find the current version at www.github.com/kotlin/anko), so the code would look like this:

```
compile "org.jetbrains.anko:anko-commons:0.10.1"
```

We would then paste this line of code into the *build.gradle* file, under the *dependencies* method. There are two *build.gradle* files on the left panel, be sure to copy this line of code into the one situated inside your app folder, **not outside of it**.

Once you are done, you will see a message at the top of your screen saying the *gradle* files have been changed and a project sync is needed. On the top right of your screen there will be a button saying 'Sync Now'. Click that and wait for the project sync to complete. If you have done this step correctly, there should be no errors when it finishes the *gradle build*.

Now we can return to the *MainActivity.kt* file. In here we are going to add a function named *changeText*. This function will change the text of the TextView to whatever we want, when we click the 'Say Hello' button.

So, in code form, the function will look like this:

═══════ code example ═══════

```
fun changeText(){
    btnSayHello.setOnClickListener{
        lblText.setText("Hello world!")
    }
}
```

Here you can see, we are setting an on-click listener for the button, and inside this on-click listener, we are programming it so that it will set the text for the *lblText* element to 'Hello world!'.

Finally, you'll want to call the *changeText* function at the end of the *onCreate* function. This is simply done by writing the name of the function and then adding an open and close bracket pair.

Your *MainActivity.kt* file should now look something like this:

─────────── code example ───────────

```kotlin
package com.example.michael.kotlinhelloworld

import android.support.v7.app.AppCompatActivity
import android.os.Bundle
import kotlinx.android.synthetic.main.activity_main.*

class MainActivity : AppCompatActivity() {

    override fun onCreate(savedInstanceState: Bundle?) {
        super.onCreate(savedInstanceState)
        setContentView(R.layout.activity_main)
        changeText()
    }

    fun changeText(){
        btnSayHello.setOnClickListener{
            lblText.setText("Hello world!")
        }
    }
}
```

The first line of the program, above, where it shows the package will be different in your version, as it will contain the details you entered at the start when creating the Android project – it'll most likely be your name.

That's it! We can now click the green play icon in the top right of the screen to run our app. In this menu, you will see any virtual devices you've made, or any physical devices you have connected to your computer. For example, I am testing with a *OnePlus 3*, and I've created a few virtual devices before:

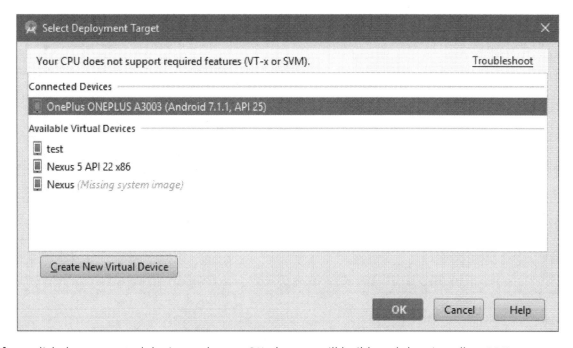

If you click the connected device and press OK, the app will build, and then install an APK on your device. If you select a virtual device and press OK, an emulator will be started and the APK will be installed on the emulator. For the purposes of this book, I encourage testing on a connected device. Here are some screenshots of the app we just built in use:

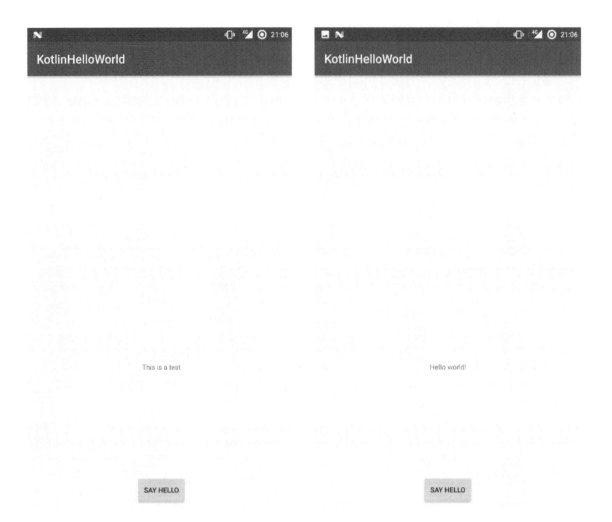

On the left, you can see what the app looked like when we first started it up, and on the right how the app looks when we have clicked the 'Say Hello' button.

You have now successfully created your first Android app in Kotlin, congratulations! In the next chapter, we will be moving onto a slightly more interesting app; *Higher or Lower*.

Chapter 4 – Higher or Lower (Your Second App)

Now we're going to move on to the more fun app development, as we know the basics of what we have to do to get an app off-the-ground. In this chapter, we are going to be developing a game named 'Higher or Lower'. Higher or Lower is a fairly straightforward game. A number is generated at random, within a range of two numbers. The user then has to guess the number in as few goes as possible. If they guess the correct answer, they win. If they don't, the game will feed back information as to whether they should guess higher or lower.

To begin, we will create a new project in Android Studio like we did for our first app. For the sake of not repeating myself and making you read a lot of stuff over again, if you do not remember how to create a new project skim over the first section of the last chapter, and instead of creating an app named 'KotlinHelloWorld', name the app 'HigherOrLower'. We will be using an empty activity again, as well as the same API version, and you can leave the name of the main activity as MainActivity.

Got that sorted? Perfect, let's continue.

Firstly, we will need to bring the Anko commons dependencies into our project, so, like we did in our first app, copy the line of code below into the dependencies method of the application's build.gradle file:

```
compile "org.jetbrains.anko:anko-commons:0.10.1"
```

Sync the project and once that has completed, we can begin our design stage.

Now what we want to do is drag a TextView onto our screen, and change the ID of the element to lblFeedback (it will give feedback on whether we should guess higher or lower), and change the text of this TextView to something like "Ready to go". We want this element's text to be larger than usual, so in the attributes menu on the right, click 'View all attributes' at the bottom of the pane. This will show you all the attributes of the element. Scroll down this list until you find 'textSize' and enter the value 30sp. You should now have something which looks like this:

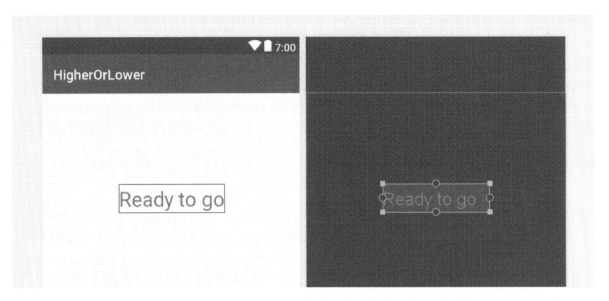

Next, we will drag a button onto the screen. We will give this button the ID of *btnGuess*, and change the text of this button to 'Guess'. You should now have something looking like this:

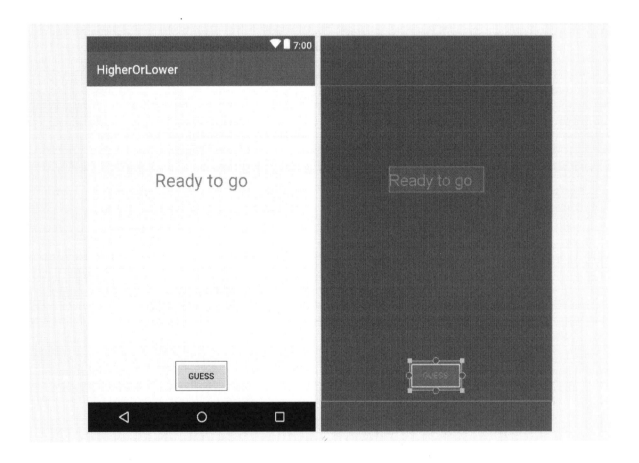

Next, we'll add a *Number* field to the screen, just above the button. We will give this field the ID *numGuess* and not set any text for it. We will, however, change the '*textAlignment*' so that the input appears in the centre of the field. Select '*center*' from the list of all attributes. You should now have something which looks like this:

Before we begin programming our app, we will want to add constraints to the elements on screen so they don't jump around. If you remember from the last chapter, we drag the circles on the sides of the elements to places on screen. Play around with them to see if you can control the constraints yourself. Remember, drag the circles on either side of an element to either side of the screen to centralise it.

You should end up with constraints looking like this:

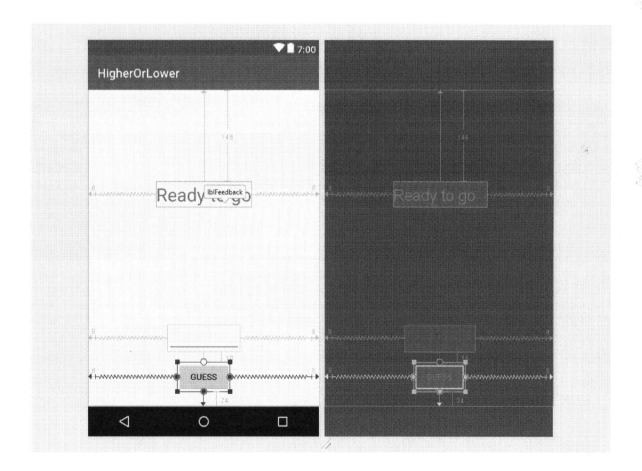

Now we can begin the programming behind the game. On the next page is the source code for the *MainActivity.kt* file, and after the code example I will explain what is happening, and what specific parts of the code means.

```
package com.example.michael.higherorlower

import android.support.v7.app.AppCompatActivity
import android.os.Bundle
import kotlinx.android.synthetic.main.activity_main.*
import java.util.*

class MainActivity : AppCompatActivity() {

    var randomNum = 0

    override fun onCreate(savedInstanceState: Bundle?) {
        super.onCreate(savedInstanceState)
        setContentView(R.layout.activity_main)

        assignRandomNumber()
        createListenerForButton()
    }

    fun generateRandomNumber(): Int{
        var random = Random()
        var min = 1
        var max = 10
        randomNum = random.nextInt(max + 1 - min) + min

        return randomNum
    }

    fun assignRandomNumber(){
        randomNum = generateRandomNumber()
    }

    fun guessNumber(){
        var numberToGuess = randomNum
        var userGuess: Int = Integer.parseInt(numGuess.getText().toString())

        checkUserGuess(userGuess, numberToGuess)
    }

    fun checkUserGuess(userGuess: Int, numberToGuess: Int){
        if(userGuess > numberToGuess) {
            lblFeedback.setText("Lower")
        } else if (userGuess < numberToGuess) {
            lblFeedback.setText("Higher")
        } else {
            lblFeedback.setText("Correct!")
        }
    }

    fun createListenerForButton(){
        btnGuess.setOnClickListener{
            guessNumber()
        }
    }
}
```

This is a fully-functioning set of code for the higher or lower game. Highlighted in yellow are some points I want to cover before we look into the functions that make up the game. Firstly, at the top, you can see we are importing *java.util.**. A star symbol usually means 'all' in computing, so we are importing all of Java's utilities, which we may need to use. We can do this because, as I've mentioned before, Kotlin and Java are 100% interoperable and so anything missing from Kotlin right now, we can pinch from Java.

The next line highlighted is a variable being initialised. This is a key thing to point out, as the variable is outside of all the functions, but it is still in the class. This makes this variable a **global variable**, and so any function can use or change its value as the program runs.

Below the variable you'll find the *onCreate* method. You will see we have added two new lines to this method, one calling the *assignRandomNumber* method, and one calling the *createListenerForButton* method. This means when the app is run, a new random number will be generated and there will be a listener for any button clicks.

The *generateRandomNumber* function returns an integer when it is called. Inside this function, a new *random* object is created (Kotlin does not use the *new* keyword). Then, a minimum and maximum set of variables are created. These act as the ranges in which the random number can be generated. Next, the *randomNum* variable which is – as we said – the global variable, is assigned a random number. Finally, the function returns a random number.

Next, we have the *assignRandomNumber* method, and this simply assigns the *randomNum* variable the random number which is generated when *generateRandomNumber* is called.

Beneath that, we have *guessNumber*. This is the method that is called whenever the button is clicked, and so it gets the *numberToGuess* from the global variable *randomNum*, and then it finds the *userGuess* from the value the user has entered into the Number field in the app. We have to turn this value into a *string* and then convert it back to an *integer* for the assignment to work, and that is what is going on in that line of code. Finally, the method calls *checkUserGuess* and gives it the parameters *userGuess* and *numberToGuess*.

The next function we have is *checkUserGuess*, which takes the *userGuess* variable, and the *numberToGuess* variable, and puts them through an *if statement* to check if they are higher, lower or equal to each other, and changes the text of the TextView based on that outcome.

Finally, we have the *createListenerForButton* function, and this simply creates an on-click listener for the button we have on screen, and when it is clicked, the *guessNumber* method will be called.

But, what if the user didn't enter anything before pressing the guess button? Well, now we need some validation. We'll keep it simple, but you can get as in-depth as you want to with validation to make it as robust as possible. What we'll do is check if the Number field is empty before calling the *guessNumber* method. If it is, we'll display a message back to the user that they should fix their error. The code for that would be situated in the *createListenerForButton* method, and look like this:

```
fun createListenerForButton(){
    btnGuess.setOnClickListener{
        if(numGuess.getText().toString().equals("")){
            toast("Please enter a number")
        } else {
            guessNumber()
        }
    }
}
```

Here we are adapting the *createListenerForButton* method, and as you can see we first check if the data entered in the Number field is empty, and in that case we display a *toast* message to the user asking them to enter a number. A *toast* is a small pop-up which displays a short sentence on the user's screen.

We will now add another activity to our app, so we can show a more exciting 'correct guess' screen.

What we want to do first is right-click our layout folder, under *res*, and select *New, Activity, Empty Activity*. We can then name the activity something like *'CorrectGuessActivity'*, and leave *'Generate Layout File'* and *'Backwards Compatibility'* checked. Do not make it a *'Launcher Activity'*.

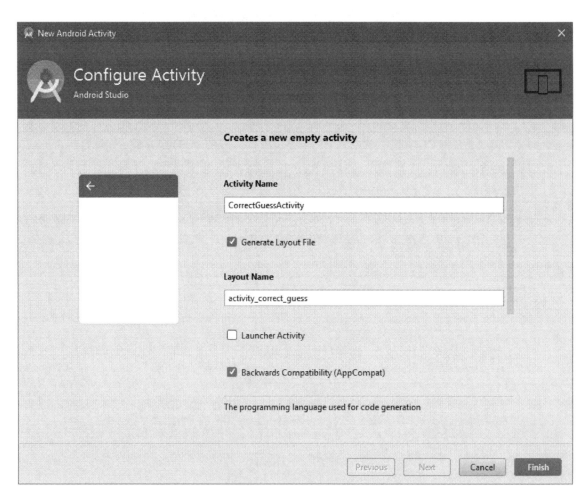

We can leave the package name as it is, but make sure the source language is in Kotlin and not Java.

Next, we are going to make this screen look a bit nicer so when we arrive at it after winning the game we feel a sense of achievement. Firstly, we will change the background colour to match the application bar. To do this, we will go into the attributes panel on the right when we have the 'ConstraintLayout' selected, and under 'View all attributes' we can find the *background* attribute. In the box for *background*, enter the value #485ECE. This is a hexadecimal code for a colour which matches the colour of the app. Once you have done this, your background colour for your app should change.

Now, we are going to add an image to the screen. You can use any image you feel is appropriate, but I encourage using one in the PNG format, and you have to name it using only lowercase letters, numbers and underscores, otherwise Android Studio may throw you some errors if you have it named with characters including spaces or uppercase letters. For this tutorial, I have used a party popper emoji image. You can download it from here: http://bit.ly/2tJvpui

When you save the image, you want to save it to the *drawables* folder of your application resources, which is usually located on your computer under: *Local Disk (C:), Users, [Your Username], AndroidStudioProjects, HigherOrLower, app, src, main, res, drawable*.

Once you have saved the image, click and drag an *ImageView* into the app's second activity screen, and then another screen will pop up asking you what image you would like to be displayed. If you have added your image correctly to the *drawables* folder, you should see the image listed at the top. Click the image and press OK. You may need to resize the ImageView using the squares at each corner of the ImageView box. Once you have completed all these steps, you should have something which looks like this:

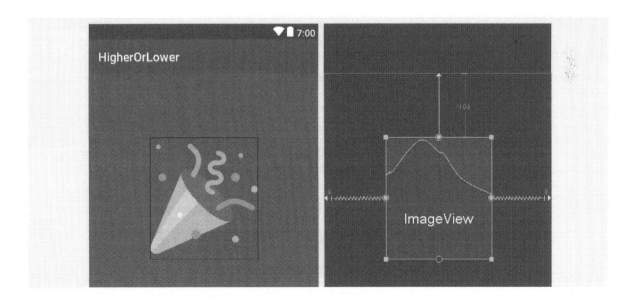

Now, give the ImageView an ID of something sensible like '*imgPartyPopper*'.

Now what we want to do is add a TextView underneath the ImageView reading something along the lines of 'Correct!'. Drag a TextView to the screen, give it the ID of '*lblCorrect*' and set the text of it to 'Correct!'. You may also want to edit the *textColor* too, so that it is white and contrasts the background more. You can find this attribute in the attributes list. Once you have added some constraints to the element, you should have something which looks like this:

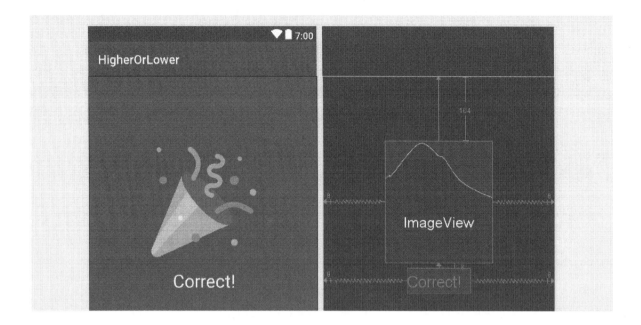

Now we will add two buttons to the bottom of the screen. One to give the user the option of playing again, and the other to give the user the option of exiting the app. So, drag two buttons to the application's screen.

Before we place constraints on them however, we are going to add a *vertical guideline* down the middle of the screen. This means that both the buttons can always have an equal amount of the screen, no matter the display size.

To do this, click the button as shown below, and select '*Add Vertical Guideline*'.

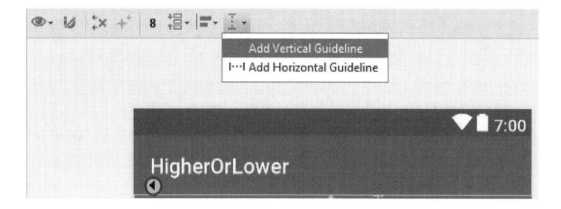

Initially, the vertical guideline will be set up to work in pixels, rather than percentage of the screen. You can change this by clicking the arrow in the circle until it turns to a '%' sign.

Now, drag the guideline to the middle of the screen, and a 50% marker will show. You can now add the constraints to the buttons so that they are either side of the guideline, and are connected to either side of the screen and guideline. You should now have something like this:

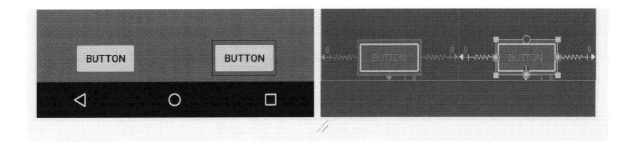

This is a good start, but we want the buttons to take up the whole 50% of the screen they can, so we will go up to the attributes menu when a button is selected, and change the inward facing arrows to jagged lines by clicking them, as shown here:

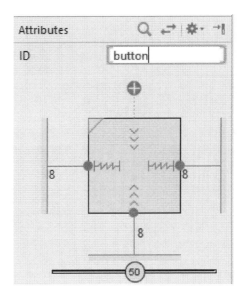

This will then have the effect of enlarging the button to take up the whole width of its constraints, like so:

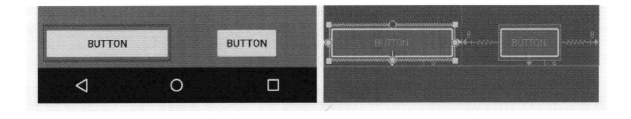

Now repeat the same step with the other button so that they match. After you have done this, give the buttons sensible IDs, like '*btnPlayAgain*' and '*btnExit*'. Then, set the text for them to match their functions, so one should read 'Play Again' and the other 'Exit'. You should end up with something like this:

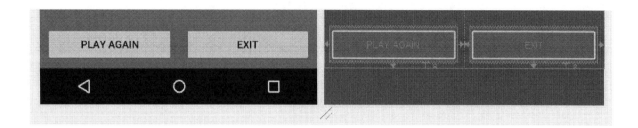

Now we have completed the design side of things, we can start setting up how we will open this activity. Firstly, you will want to open the *AndroidManifest.xml* file located in the project directory on the left panel. You will see there are two activities, but only the main activity has an *intent filter*. What we want to do is have another intent filter, but for the second activity. The code for this will look like:

================= code example =================

```xml
<?xml version="1.0" encoding="utf-8"?>
<manifest xmlns:android="http://schemas.android.com/apk/res/android"
    package="com.example.michael.higherorlower">

    <application
        android:allowBackup="true"
        android:icon="@mipmap/ic_launcher"
        android:label="@string/app_name"
        android:roundIcon="@mipmap/ic_launcher_round"
        android:supportsRtl="true"
        android:theme="@style/AppTheme">
        <activity android:name=".MainActivity">
            <intent-filter>
                <action android:name="android.intent.action.MAIN" />

                <category android:name="android.intent.category.LAUNCHER" />
            </intent-filter>
        </activity>
        <activity
            android:name=".CorrectGuessActivity">
            <intent-filter>
                <action android:name="[YOUR PACKAGE NAME]" />

                <category android:name="android.intent.category.DEFAULT" />
            </intent-filter>
        </activity>
    </application>

</manifest>
```

I have highlighted in yellow an area where you will need to put the package name from your second activity. You can find it by going into the code version of the '*activity_correct_guess.xml*' file, and it will be shown on the line regarding '*tools:context*'. All you need to do is simply copy and paste that package name into the highlighted yellow space.

So for example, the line of code in my second activity's XML file reads:

```
tools:context="com.example.michael.higherorlower.CorrectGuessActivity"
```

So, the line of code in my Android manifest file will read:

```
<action android:name="com.example.michael.higherorlower.CorrectGuessActivity" />
```

Now that we have the second activity linked in properly, we can go back to our main activity's Kotlin code, and perform some small adjustments.

Firstly, we want to add a new function, called '*openCorrectGuessScreen*'. This will open the second activity for us, using an *Intent*. An example for this code can be seen below:

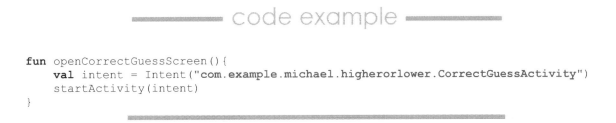

```
fun openCorrectGuessScreen(){
    val intent = Intent("com.example.michael.higherorlower.CorrectGuessActivity")
    startActivity(intent)
}
```

Here, we create a new intent and link it to our second activity (the package name we used slightly earlier), and then we call a built-in function called '*startActivity*', and pass it the parameter which is our intent.

Next, we need something to call this function. So, where we previously had an *if statement* block which changed the text of the TextView on the main activity screen to 'higher', 'lower' or 'correct', we will adapt it so that when the answer is correct, we call the function to open the correct guess screen. Here's an example of how the code would look:

```
fun checkUserGuess(userGuess: Int, numberToGuess: Int){
    if(userGuess > numberToGuess) {
        lblFeedback.setText("Lower")
    } else if (userGuess < numberToGuess) {
        lblFeedback.setText("Higher")
    } else {
        lblFeedback.setText("Correct!")
        openCorrectGuessScreen()
    }
}
```

I have highlighted where we have added the call to the *openCorrectGuessScreen* function. So now, when we make a correct guess, it will open our second activity.

Now what we need to do is add some code to our second activity's Kotlin file. So, open '*CorrectGuessActivity.kt*' as we need to add functionality for the buttons we placed on screen.

Firstly, we will be adding the '*playAgain*' function. This will allow us to – when the button is clicked – return to the main game screen, and have another game. The code for this looks like:

```
fun playAgain(){
    btnPlayAgain.setOnClickListener{
        val intent = Intent("[YOUR MAIN ACTIVITY'S PACKAGE NAME]")
        startActivity(intent)
    }
}
```

In this function, we are setting an on-click listener for our *btnPlayAgain* button, and inside this listener, we are launching the first activity again. You will see in the code above that in the Intent parameters, I have not filled in where your main activity's package name should be. You can find this package name in the '*activity_main.xml*' text code, in the same place we found the second activity's package name last time.

The other function we need to add is '*exitGame*'. This will allow the user to exit the game when they click the button on the second activity's screen. An example of this code is here:

```
fun exitGame(){
    btnExit.setOnClickListener{
        this.finishAffinity()
    }
}
```

In this function, we are setting an on-click listener for the 'btnExit' button. In this listener, we have a line of code which finishes the current activity, as well as all other activities below it of the same affinity[2]. This means our application should exit without jumping back to the main activity.

Now what we need to do is call both the functions we just made from the *onCreate* function, which will mean when the activity starts up, there will be on-click listeners set up to listen for clicks, and perform their actions accordingly. To do this, we edit the *onCreate* function in the following way:

```
override fun onCreate(savedInstanceState: Bundle?) {
    super.onCreate(savedInstanceState)
    setContentView(R.layout.activity_correct_guess)

    playAgain()
    exitGame()
}
```

Here you can see I have highlighted the two lines of code, which simply call the functions we just made. That is all that is needed to give the buttons we made on our second activity's screen their required functionality.

We have now finished creating our Higher or Lower application. You should test your application now to check you have not missed any steps. It is always good practice to test run your application after each incremental change you make to your design or code, so you can identify exactly where a problem may have occurred.

Chapter 5 – BMI Calculator (Your Third App)

The third and final app we will build is a BMI (Body Mass Index) calculator. For those of you who aren't familiar with BMI, it is a commonly used scale to measure how healthy a person is, depending on their height and weight. You calculate your BMI through this equation, supplied by the NHS[3]:

$$\textbf{(weight (kg) / height (m)) / height (m)}$$

What we need to do first is create a new project in Android Studio, like we did with the other apps we have built. Again, to save you reading a lot of content over again here, if you do not remember how to create a project, refer to the first chapter. We will name the application *'BMICalculator'*, remain using the *API 16: Android 4.1 (Jelly Bean)*, and we will select an empty activity. We will also leave the first activity named *'MainActivity'*.

Ready to go? Fantastic.

The first thing to do is add this line of code to the *dependencies* method in your application's *build.gradle* file. Remember, the version of *Anko* commons may have changed since this book published, so be sure to compile with the latest build number (which can be found here: www.github.com/kotlin/anko):

```
compile "org.jetbrains.anko:anko-commons:0.10.1"
```

Once the project has synced, we can begin the first design stage of our application. Open the *'activity_main.xml'* file in the Design view, as we'll need to place some elements on-screen. We are going to need two *TextViews*, two *Number (Decimal)* fields and a button, laid out like so:

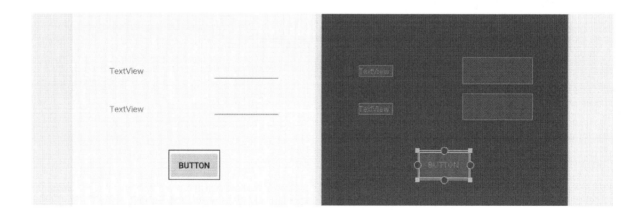

Now, name the TextViews something like *'lblWeight'* and *'lblHeight'*. Name the Number (Decimal) fields *'numWeight'* and *'numHeight'*. Name the Button *'btnCalculateBMI'*.

Next, change the text of the elements so they read something like this:

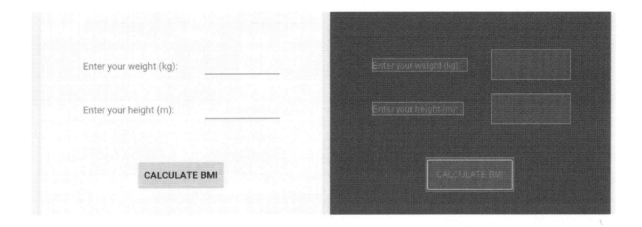

Now you need to add some constraints to your elements to ensure they don't jump around the screen. You should end up with some that look like this:

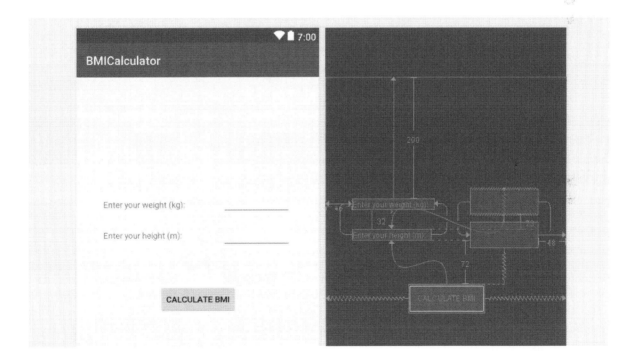

I'll let you in on a pro-tip which sometimes saves you a lot of time. If you look at the menu above your design, you will see an icon of two stars. This is the '*Infer Constraints*' button, and when you click it, Android Studio will try to sort out your constraints for you. It doesn't always work, but if you are getting frustrated at constraints not doing what you want them to, this may save you a few hours/your sanity.

Now what we want to do is create another activity for our application, like we did in the last chapter. So, right-click the *layout* folder user *res*, click *New, Activity, Empty Activity*. Name this activity something like '*BMIResultsScreen*'. Click finish.

On this activity, we want to add three TextView elements, and two Buttons in this sort of format:

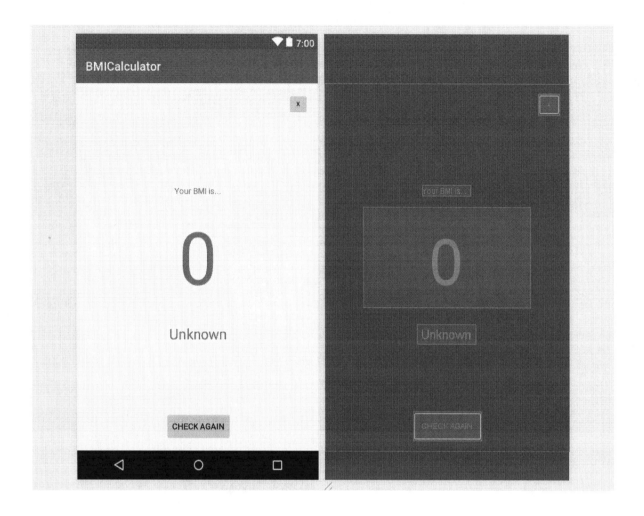

Name the top TextView something like '*lblYourBMI*', the TextView below '*lblBMIResult*' and the final TextView '*lblBMIResultCategory*'. Name the button in the top right corner '*btnExit*' and the button at the bottom '*btnCheckAgain*'.

As you can see, I have changed the '*textSize*', '*textAlignment*' and '*textColor*' of the middle TextView, so that it stands out from the rest, as this is where our main result will be when we run the app.

Now, place some constraints on the elements. You should end up with something like this (done via inferring constraints):

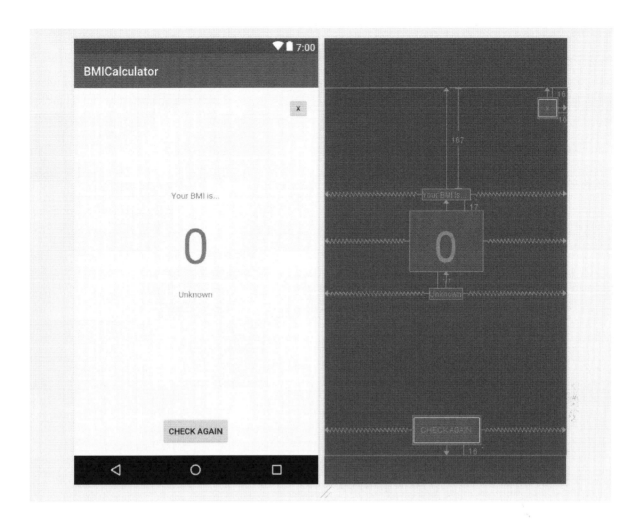

Now, like in the last chapter, we want to make this activity accessible from the main activity. So, we need to perform the same changes we did to our 'AndroidManifest.xml' file as we did in the last chapter, where we copied the *intent filter* from the main activity, and then changed the name to the second activity's package name, and the category to 'DEFAULT' rather than 'LAUNCHER'. Your manifest file should now look like this:

```xml
<?xml version="1.0" encoding="utf-8"?>
<manifest xmlns:android="http://schemas.android.com/apk/res/android"
    package="com.example.michael.bmicalculator">

    <application
        android:allowBackup="true"
        android:icon="@mipmap/ic_launcher"
        android:label="@string/app_name"
        android:roundIcon="@mipmap/ic_launcher_round"
        android:supportsRtl="true"
        android:theme="@style/AppTheme">
        <activity android:name=".MainActivity">
            <intent-filter>
                <action android:name="android.intent.action.MAIN" />

                <category android:name="android.intent.category.LAUNCHER" />
            </intent-filter>
        </activity>
        <activity android:name=".BMIResultsScreen">
            <intent-filter>
                <action
android:name="com.example.michael.bmicalculator.BMIResultsScreen" />

                <category android:name="android.intent.category.DEFAULT" />
            </intent-filter>
        </activity>
    </application>

</manifest>
```

The areas highlighted show where you should switch out my package name with your package name. The first should be your general package name, while the other should be the package name found in the 'tools:context' line of your second activity's XML code.

Now we have this step completed, we can get back to the Kotlin code.

Go back to the 'MainActivity.kt' file. In here we will need to add two new functions, one for calculating the BMI based on the user input, and one to set an on-click listener for the button on the main activity's screen. The code for this would look like:

```
package com.example.michael.bmicalculator

import android.content.Intent
import android.support.v7.app.AppCompatActivity
import android.os.Bundle
import kotlinx.android.synthetic.main.activity_main.*

class MainActivity : AppCompatActivity() {

    override fun onCreate(savedInstanceState: Bundle?) {
        super.onCreate(savedInstanceState)
        setContentView(R.layout.activity_main)

        setOnClickListenerForButton()
    }

    fun calculateBMI(): Double{
        var weight: Double = (numWeight.getText().toString().toDouble())
        var height: Double = (numHeight.getText().toString().toDouble())

        var calculatedBMI = (((weight / height) / height))

        return calculatedBMI
    }

    fun setOnClickListenerForButton(){
        btnCalculateBMI.setOnClickListener{
            val intent =
Intent("com.example.michael.bmicalculator.BMIResultsScreen")
            intent.putExtra("BMIResult", calculateBMI())
            startActivity(intent)
        }
    }
}
```

Here we can see the 'MainActivity.kt' file's code. I have highlighted where your code should be different (e.g. relating to your own package names). You can see we have a function named 'calculateBMI'. This returns a *Double* value (a value with decimal points), and it takes the weight and height from the app's *Number (Decimal)* fields, and then performs a calculation on them to make the BMI value. This value is then returned. Next, we see the 'setOnClickListenerForButton' method. This – as the name suggests – sets an on-click listener for the 'btnCalculateBMI' button. If the button is clicked, an *Intent* with the parameter of our second activity's package is run. What you'll also notice is that we are now passing some information from this activity to the next activity, using the Intent. We give the value we are passing a name, and then pass the actual value. We are passing the 'calculateBMI' method as it returns a Double value. Finally, we start the activity. You'll also notice that we have called this method from the *onCreate* function, to finish setting up the on-click listener.

Now we need to turn our attention to the second activity's code. You can see this here:

```kotlin
package com.example.michael.bmicalculator

import android.content.Intent
import android.support.v7.app.AppCompatActivity
import android.os.Bundle
import kotlinx.android.synthetic.main.activity_bmiresults_screen.*
import java.text.DecimalFormat

class BMIResultsScreen : AppCompatActivity() {

    override fun onCreate(savedInstanceState: Bundle?) {
        super.onCreate(savedInstanceState)
        setContentView(R.layout.activity_bmiresults_screen)

        showBMIResult()
        findBMICategory()

        setExitListener()
        setCheckAgainListener()
    }

    fun showBMIResult(){
        var decFormat = DecimalFormat("#.#")
        var formattedBMI =
decFormat.format(getIntent().getExtras().getDouble("BMIResult"))
        lblBMIResult.setText(formattedBMI.toString())
    }

    fun findBMICategory(){
        var categoryOfBMI = "Unknown"
        var resultBMI = getIntent().getExtras().getDouble("BMIResult")

        if(resultBMI < 15){
            categoryOfBMI = "Very Severely Underweight"
        } else if(resultBMI in 15..16){
            categoryOfBMI = "Severely Underweight"
        } else if(resultBMI > 16 && resultBMI <= 18.5){
            categoryOfBMI = "Underweight"
        } else if(resultBMI > 18.5 && resultBMI <= 25){
            categoryOfBMI = "Normal (Healthy Weight)"
        } else if(resultBMI in 25..30){
            categoryOfBMI = "Overweight"
        } else if(resultBMI in 30..35){
            categoryOfBMI = "Moderately Obese"
        } else if(resultBMI in 35..40){
            categoryOfBMI = "Severely Obese"
        } else if(resultBMI >= 40){
            categoryOfBMI = "Very Severely Obese"
        }

        lblBMIResultCategory.setText(categoryOfBMI)
    }

    fun setExitListener(){
        btnExit.setOnClickListener {
            this.finishAffinity()
        }
    }
```

```
fun setCheckAgainListener(){
    btnCheckAgain.setOnClickListener{
        val intent = Intent("com.example.michael.bmicalculator.MainActivity")
        startActivity(intent)
    }
  }
}
```

Our first new method here is the '*showBMIResult*' function. Here, we use a class named *DecimalFormat* which helps us to only show one decimal point for our calculation. We then get the BMI number which was calculated by the other activity by getting the *extras* from the Intent, and specifying the key of the value we want. Finally, we set the text of the '*lblBMIResult*' element to a formatted, *String* version of the BMI number.

The next method we have is '*findBMICategory*'. This takes the value of the BMI result from the previous activity, and then performs an *if statement* to check where the user is on the spectrum. Most of the *if statement* uses *ranges*, which are a nifty feature of Kotlin. There are a few *else if statements* which have to use the older method due to the BMI model changing category at 18.5, a floating-point number instead of an integer. Kotlin's ranges like integers (however floating-point ranges have been introduced in Kotlin version 1.1). When the category has been found, the variable '*categoryOfBMI*' is set a value and then this value is set as the '*lblBMIResultCategory*' text.

Below this method, we have '*setExitListener*' and '*setCheckAgainListener*'. These both set up on-click listeners for the buttons we used in our app, similarly to what we did in the last chapter.

After you've implemented that code, that's it for our third and final app, and this chapter. It is worth me noting that even though the BMI is widely used in the world of fitness, it isn't a sure sign of a person's health. A person may be very muscly, which causes them to weigh more, which makes BMI show their BMI category as more severe than it should be. The BMI tests can also depend on a person's age or gender, and their lifestyle. Here we built a simple version of the test, but if you feel like a challenge, I encourage you to investigate it more and possibly build upon the application we've made already.

Chapter 6 – Extras

Now we are going to turn our attention away from Kotlin slightly, and look at a few other aspects of app development which I think you may find useful when building upon the skills you've picked up in the last few chapters. We will explore *constraints* a bit more, while finding out how you can set up layouts for different screen orientations. We will also look into how you can set your application's icon to something more unique than Android's default icon.

Designing for a different screen orientation

When you are building your application, you may wish to not only use it in portrait mode, but also landscape mode on your device. The problem is; this whole time we have been developing our app and applying constraints in the portrait orientation, with no thought about how it would appear if someone changed the orientation of their screen. Thankfully, in Android Studio you can develop your applications for different orientations.

We will be using the last app we created – the BMI calculator – as an example. So, navigate to the *'activity_main.xml'* file of your BMI calculator app. In this design view, we see a button in the menu above our application's design screen, to the right of the *'Language'* button, looking like this:

Click this button, and select *'Create Landscape Variation'*. When you do this, another file will open, which reads *'land\activity_main.xml'*, indicating this is the landscape orientation version of the main activity. You will also probably see that the elements that were perfectly placed on-screen in portrait mode are now not-so-perfect in landscape. This means we made the right decision to create a landscape version of our layout, as we can fix this issue!

Simply begin dragging the elements around the screen until you can see them all (note some may not be visible as the constraints will be pushing the elements out of view). Once we can see all the elements, we can start deciding how constraints should be put in place in order to keep our design stable. You may find that the constraints we originally created are fine in this set up. If that's the case, perfect. Test your app on your device and check that it looks how you'd want it to in the landscape orientation.

However, if the constraints we had previously are not suitable, we can remove all constraints by clicking the button to the left of the *'Infer Constraints'* button. This may make some elements change their size. Don't panic, this is normal, we just have to scale them down to the size we desire. This is done via clicking and dragging the boxes at the corner of the element we have selected until we are satisfied with its size. An example can be seen here:

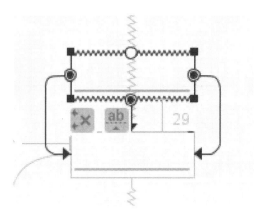

Now, once we have set up all our elements in their correct place and size, we can either add constraints manually, or opt to infer the constraints (remember the button in the menu above the design with two stars?). As inferring constraints is a lot simpler, we will choose this first, and test run our app. Here are the constraints inferred in my case (your constraints may differ):

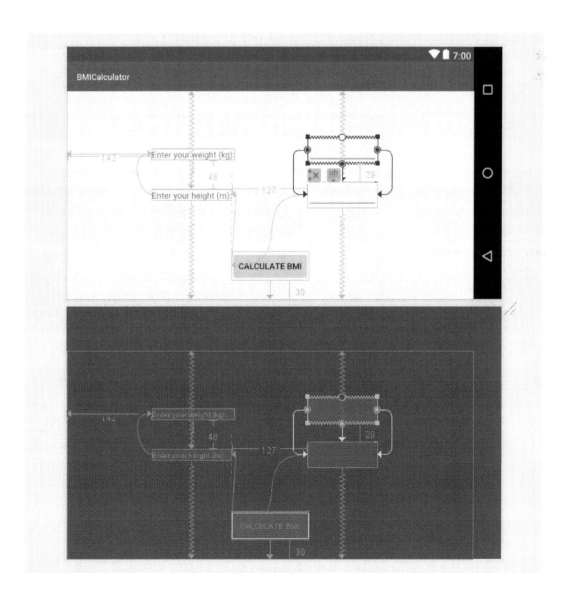

Below is what the app looked like when tested on my test device, a *OnePlus 3*:

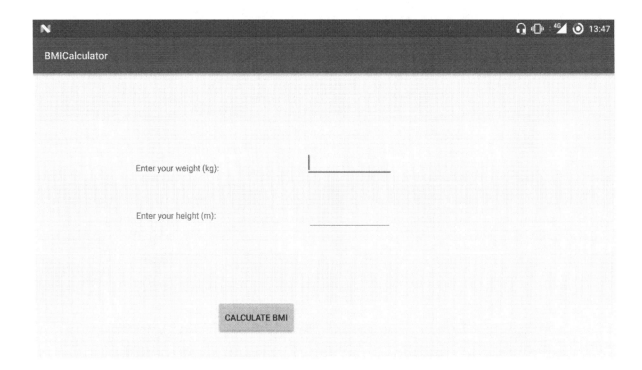

Now, we can see here that although all elements are on screen, they are not centred and so the design looks quite amateur. To fix this, we can use a vertical guideline, like we did in chapter 4. If we place the vertical guideline in the centre of the screen, and click the arrow in the circle until it turns into a percentage sign, we can now base our constraints off of that, as it will act as a marker for the middle of the screen.

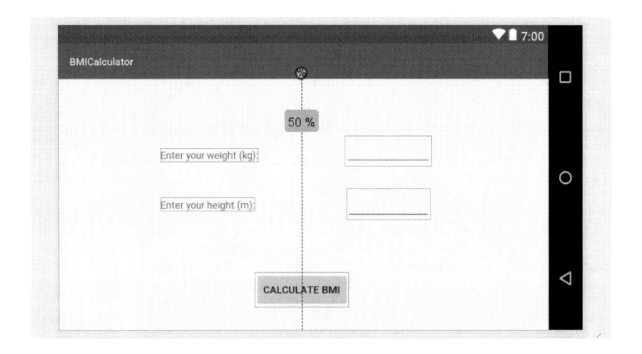

So now, if we infer constraints again, we will see that a lot of them have attached to the central guideline. Now we should test the app again on our physical device to see how it looks. Here is the result:

Now we can see that the elements we set up are perfectly aligned in the centre and so make the app feel and look much more premium and well-built.

If you'd like a challenge, try creating a landscape version of the second activity of the app, based upon the skills we used to create this version.

Using your own app icon

When you come to building your own app, with a view of releasing it on the Google Play Store, or just keeping it for personal uses, you will likely want to make it unique by adding a custom app icon. Luckily, this is fairly straightforward in Android Studio.

Firstly, we need an application icon to use. For the purpose of this tutorial, I will direct you to a very good tool when designing Android app icons, and that is *Android Asset Studio*, created by Roman Nurik of Google. Here's a link to it: http://bit.ly/2vbmXbn

The icon I created looks like this, however feel free to make any design you like:

Save your icon with a name prefixed by 'ic_', as it is common practice when developing for Android to save your icon files with that prefix. I have named my icon 'ic_launcher' as that is the default name for application launcher icons. The files you download will automatically be in a PNG format for us.

Now what you want to do is go back into Android Studio, right-click your *app* folder, select *New*, then select *Image Asset*. From here a window will open showing some default app icon settings. You want to click the '*Image*' radio button under '*Source Asset*', and in the path, select the location of your image that you downloaded. Select the xxxhdpi version. Simply click next, and you will be presented with a screen stating that you are overwriting some files. This is fine, as this means we are replacing the old icon design with our new one. Click finish, and you're done. Run the app again on your test device and you will see it now has an application icon in your menu!

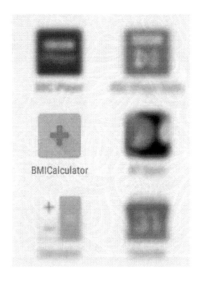

Chapter 7 – Conclusion

We made it! I would like to say congratulations and good work on creating your first few apps for Android in the Kotlin language. Looking back on what you've done, you will have picked up the skills to:

- Build an app from scratch

- Create different activities for your apps

- Link those activities together

- Send data between activities

- Understand and utilise constraints with different elements

- Use images in your apps

- Write your own Kotlin functions

- Develop apps for different screen orientations

- Create and change app icons

You should be very proud of yourself for the effort and time you have put in to learning these key skills, and exposing yourself to the new-ish programming language; Kotlin. From here, I advise you to grow even more curious about the language and developing apps for Android. There are no limits what you can achieve in the future with the invaluable skills you have just picked up.

I very much hope you have enjoyed the book, and if you feel like you'd like to learn more of the basics of Kotlin, you can check out my other book on Amazon – *Kotlin Development for Beginners (with Code Examples)*, available on Kindle and in paperback. Here's a link: http://bit.ly/kotlin-book

I wish you the very best of luck in the future for your next application developments.

The source code for the apps we made is available online here: http://bit.ly/2viUyzB

References

1. Kotlin. (2017). *FAQ - Kotlin Programming Language*. [online] Available at: https://kotlinlang.org/docs/reference/faq.html [Accessed 27 Jul. 2017].

2. Android Developers (2017). Activity. [online] Available at: https://developer.android.com/reference/android/app/Activity.html [Accessed 28 Jul. 2017].

3. NHS. (2017). How can I work out my body mass index (BMI)? - Health questions - NHS Choices. [online] Available at: http://www.nhs.uk/chq/Pages/how-can-i-work-out-my-bmi.aspx?CategoryID=51&SubCategoryID=165 [Accessed 31 Jul. 2017].

Made in the USA
Middletown, DE
27 January 2018